Collins

Children's Picture Atlas of the Stars

Tom Kerss

Illustrated by Steve Evans

Published by Collins
An imprint of HarperCollins*Publishers*
Westerhill Road
Bishopbriggs
Glasgow
G64 2QT

HarperCollins*Publishers*
Macken House, 39/40 Mayor Street Upper, Dublin 1, D01 C9W8, Ireland

collins.co.uk

First published 2023

© HarperCollins*Publishers* 2023

Collins® is a registered trademark of HarperCollins*Publishers* Ltd.

Text © Tom Kerss
Illustrations by Steve Evans

Publisher: Michelle l'Anson
Project manager: Rachel Allegro
Design: Steve Evans, James Hunter and Kevin Robbins
Cover: Steve Evans and James Hunter
Production: Ilaria Rovera

A catalogue record for this book is available from the British Library.

ISBN: 9780008621933

Printed by Oriental Press, UAE.

10 9 8 7 6 5 4 3 2 1

Collins

Children's
Picture
Atlas
of the
Stars

Tom Kerss
Illustrated by Steve Evans

Soar through the night sky

For thousands of years, people have used the stars to help them navigate while travelling. They have seen different patterns in the stars and told stories about them.

Over the years, the stars have been mapped by many explorers from different cultures. These maps of the night sky are known as star charts. They show all the common patterns of stars, called constellations.

There are 88 constellations in total. The star charts in this book map the whole sky. As you journey through them, you'll learn about the constellations and the science, history and myths surrounding them.

Imagine all the stars and constellations being placed in a big sphere around the Earth, called the Celestial Sphere. The stars you see depend upon where you are in the world, and the time of year.

Northern Polar Skies

Northern Skies
(Northern hemisphere)

Shared Skies
(Equator - the imaginary line that goes around the middle of the sphere)

Southern Skies
(Southern hemisphere)

Southern Polar Skies

Each star chart in this book shows a different part of the sky. Sometimes you'll see a constellation on more than one chart as the charts overlap and sometimes they will appear upside down.

5

Hounds and Horns

Ursa Minor

Boötes

Canes Venatici

Asterion and Chara are the names of these two hunting dogs, although originally, these stars formed a club or other weapon held by Boötes (the herdsman).

Coma Berenices

Leo Minor

Leo Minor, the little lion (or lion cub) is much less ancient than the brighter Leo (the lion) and is tricky to find among the large creatures surrounding it.

Leo

Cancer

Regulus

Crater

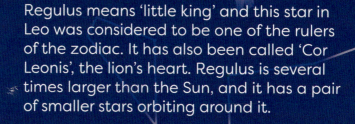

Regulus means 'little king' and this star in Leo was considered to be one of the rulers of the zodiac. It has also been called 'Cor Leonis', the lion's heart. Regulus is several times larger than the Sun, and it has a pair of smaller stars orbiting around it.

What do you think Crater is?

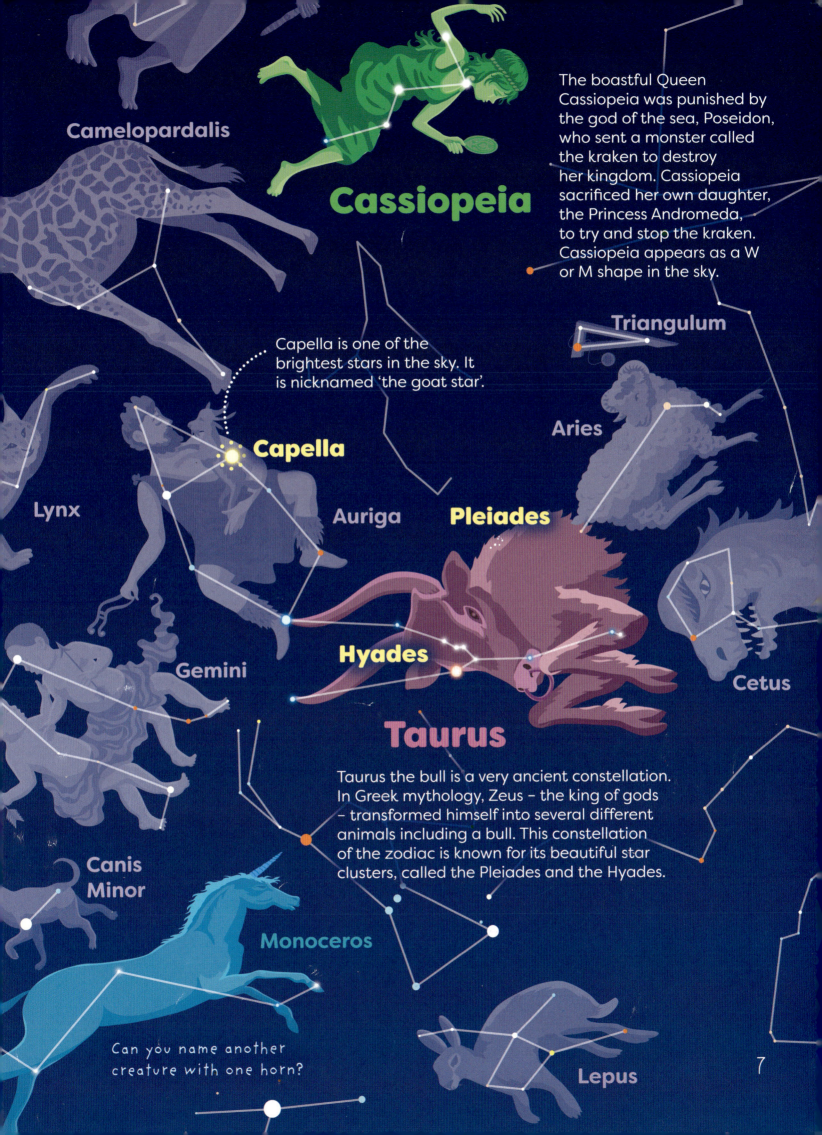

Cameleopardalis

Cassiopeia

The boastful Queen Cassiopeia was punished by the god of the sea, Poseidon, who sent a monster called the kraken to destroy her kingdom. Cassiopeia sacrificed her own daughter, the Princess Andromeda, to try and stop the kraken. Cassiopeia appears as a W or M shape in the sky.

Capella is one of the brightest stars in the sky. It is nicknamed 'the goat star'.

Triangulum

Capella

Aries

Lynx

Auriga

Pleiades

Gemini

Hyades

Cetus

Taurus

Taurus the bull is a very ancient constellation. In Greek mythology, Zeus – the king of gods – transformed himself into several different animals including a bull. This constellation of the zodiac is known for its beautiful star clusters, called the Pleiades and the Hyades.

Canis Minor

Monoceros

Can you name another creature with one horn?

Lepus

7

The Zodiac

Each year, as the Earth moves around (orbits) the Sun, the Sun also appears to move through the stars. It crosses in front of twelve constellations, one by one, which we call the constellations of the zodiac. It also crosses a thirteenth star pattern called Ophiuchus.

AQUARIUS

PISCES

ARIES

TAURUS

GEMINI

CANCER

In ancient times, stargazers used the stars of the zodiac like a calendar, which helped them track the changing seasons. They would look to see which stars were visible after sunset in the west, or before sunrise in the east to see the progress of the year. For example, the stars of Virgo used to rise in the east before sunrise in the late summer, just ahead of the time to harvest the grain.

LEO

VIRGO

LIBRA

SCORPIUS

SAGITTARIUS

CAPRICORNUS

Birds and Bears

Cepheus

Cygnus

Cygnus the swan is said to represent many characters, including the god Zeus and the hero Orpheus. It is a large constellation whose brightest stars form a shape called the Northern Cross.

Draco

Vulpecula

Lyra **Vega**

Equuleus

Delphinus

Sagitta

Vega, a star in Lyra, is an important star. Astronomers once compared the brightness of all other stars to Vega. This brightness scale is still used today.

Aquila

Capricornus

In a Greek myth, Zeus sent the eagle that carried his thunderbolts to kidnap a boy called Ganymede and bring him to Mount Olympus. The eagle, named Aquila, is one of several birds amongst the constellations.

Sagittarius

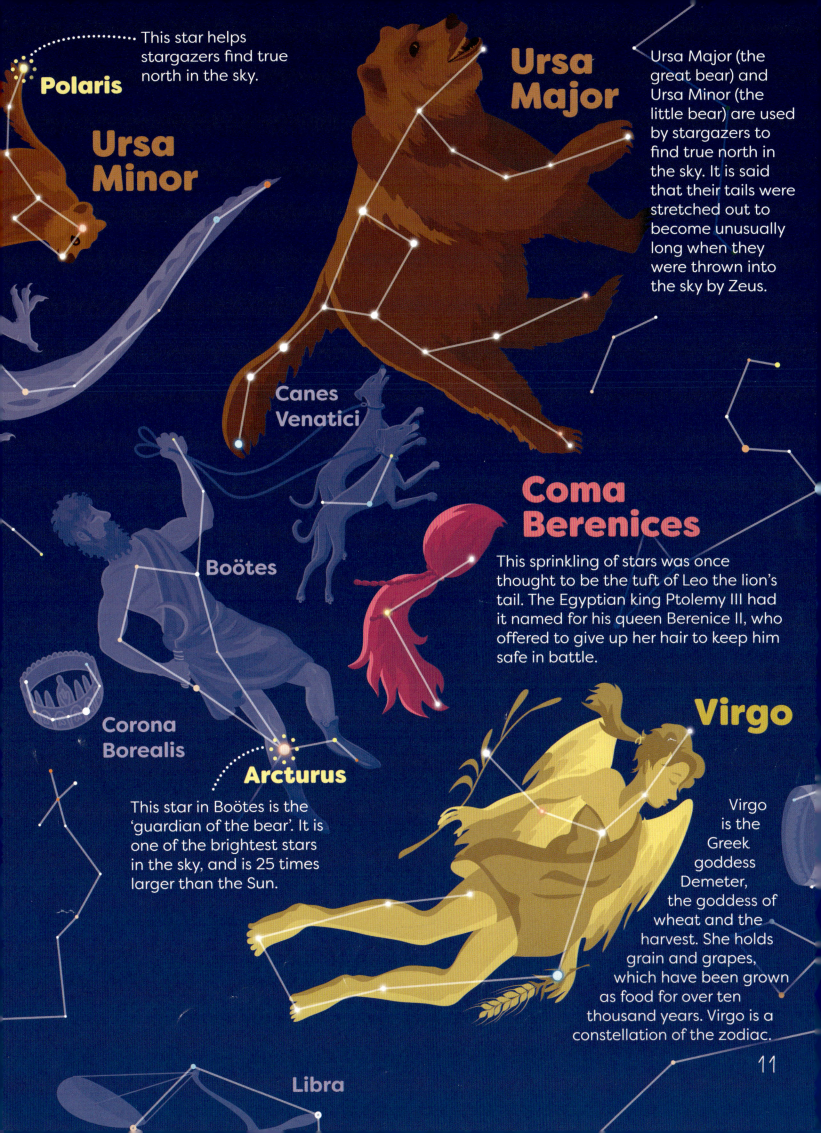

Polaris

This star helps stargazers find true north in the sky.

Ursa Minor

Ursa Major

Ursa Major (the great bear) and Ursa Minor (the little bear) are used by stargazers to find true north in the sky. It is said that their tails were stretched out to become unusually long when they were thrown into the sky by Zeus.

Canes Venatici

Boötes

Coma Berenices

This sprinkling of stars was once thought to be the tuft of Leo the lion's tail. The Egyptian king Ptolemy III had it named for his queen Berenice II, who offered to give up her hair to keep him safe in battle.

Corona Borealis

Virgo

Arcturus

This star in Boötes is the 'guardian of the bear'. It is one of the brightest stars in the sky, and is 25 times larger than the Sun.

Virgo is the Greek goddess Demeter, the goddess of wheat and the harvest. She holds grain and grapes, which have been grown as food for over ten thousand years. Virgo is a constellation of the zodiac.

Libra

11

The Pole Bears

Polaris

Ursa Minor

In the northern hemisphere, stargazers use the star Polaris, also called the Pole Star or the North Star, to find the direction of true north in the sky. Polaris is in the tip of the tail of Ursa Minor (the little bear). It is very close to the north pole of the sky, which is called the North Celestial Pole.

It's easy to find Polaris using a pattern called the 'Plough' (also known as the 'Big Dipper') made up of bright stars in the back and tail of Ursa Major (the great bear). Two of these stars, called Merak and Dubhe, are known as the Pointers. They point the way towards Polaris. As the night goes by, all the stars in the sky trace circles around Polaris. Polaris itself also makes a little circle, but it is hard to notice it moving.

Ursa Major

Dubhe

Merak

The Plough

Monsters and Music

Auriga

Auriga's name means 'charioteer' (or 'chariot driver') but he is usually seen to be holding a goat. The goat is called Amalthea, and is the foster-mother of the king of the gods, Zeus.

Gemini

Cassiopeia

Perseus

Algol

Nicknamed the 'Demon Star', Algol is the head of the mythical creature Medusa, which is found in the constellation Perseus. Looking into Medusa's eyes would turn you to stone!

Triangulum

Aries

In Greek legend, Aries the ram (or sheep) had a golden fleece, which was kept in a temple in a distant land called Colchis. A hero named Jason led a group of sailors called the Argonauts on a quest to fetch the fleece so that he could become ruler. This story has been told for nearly three thousand years.

Andromeda

Pisces

Cetus

Which animals could have been mistaken for sea monsters?

Fornax

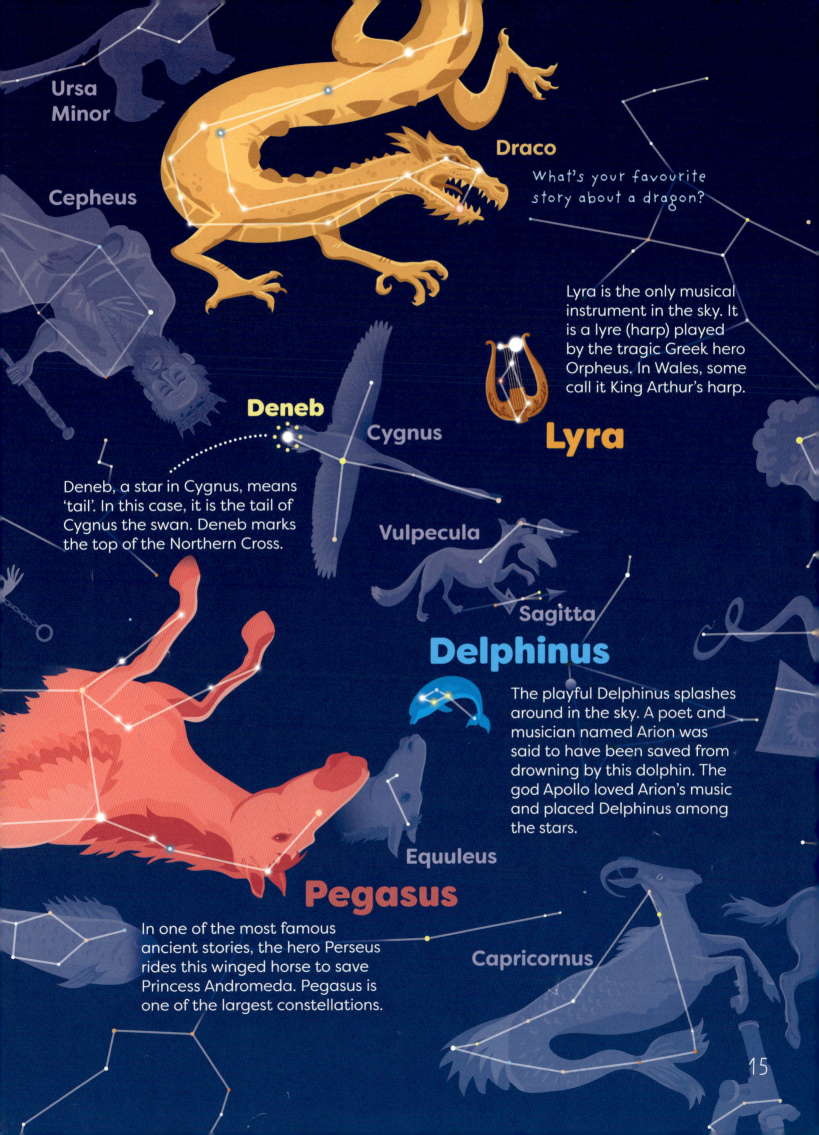

Ursa Minor

Cepheus

Draco

What's your favourite story about a dragon?

Lyra is the only musical instrument in the sky. It is a lyre (harp) played by the tragic Greek hero Orpheus. In Wales, some call it King Arthur's harp.

Lyra

Deneb

Cygnus

Deneb, a star in Cygnus, means 'tail'. In this case, it is the tail of Cygnus the swan. Deneb marks the top of the Northern Cross.

Vulpecula

Sagitta

Delphinus

The playful Delphinus splashes around in the sky. A poet and musician named Arion was said to have been saved from drowning by this dolphin. The god Apollo loved Arion's music and placed Delphinus among the stars.

Equuleus

Pegasus

In one of the most famous ancient stories, the hero Perseus rides this winged horse to save Princess Andromeda. Pegasus is one of the largest constellations.

Capricornus

15

Legendary Beasts

Our ancestors often told tales of strange and mythical creatures. Some of these creatures can be found among the constellations, which remind us of the long tradition of storytelling using the stars. In many parts of the world, this tradition continues today as legends are passed down by parents to their children. You may even recognise some of these legendary beasts from stories you've heard.

Phoenix - immortal bird

hot wings

Feathers

sharp beak

claws

FIERY TAIL

Nest of flames

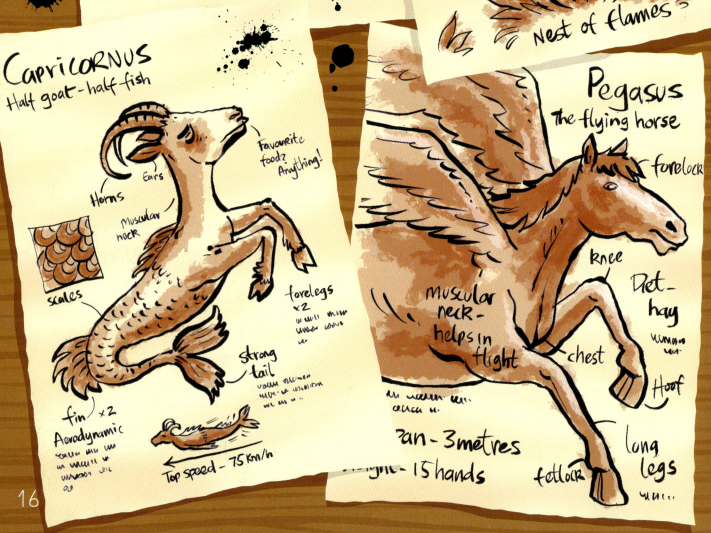

CapriCORNUS
Half goat - half fish

Horns

Ears

Muscular neck

scales

Favourite food? Anything!

forelegs x2

strong tail

fin x2
Aerodynamic

Top speed - 75 Km/h

Pegasus
The flying horse

forelock

knee

muscular neck - helps in flight

Diet - hay

chest

Hoof

...an - 3 metres

...15 hands

fetlock

long legs

Brothers and Big Cat

Lynx

Leo Minor

Pollux

Coma Berenices

Cancer

Leo

Leo is a large lion who attacked a Greek village called Nemea. The king asked the hero Hercules to slay this lion as the first of his twelve tasks.

Virgo

Monoceros

Monoceros the unicorn is one of many mythical beasts in the night sky. This constellation is faint, but it is easy to find between Orion and his two dogs, Canis Major and Canis Minor.

Spica

The brightest star in Virgo is actually two stars very close together. The name Spica means 'ear of grain' and it marks the wheat that Virgo holds in her hand.

Pyxis

Antlia

What do you think Antlia looks like?

Centaurus

Vela

Castor and Pollux are the Gemini twin brothers (and the names of the two stars seen in the brothers' heads). In some legends, they travelled everywhere together doing heroic deeds, riding upon a pair of white horses.

Castor

Gemini

The red eye of Taurus the bull is a giant star 45 times bigger than the Sun! Its name means the 'follower' because this star seems to follow the Pleiades star cluster across the sky.

Aries

Pleiades

Aldebaran

Orion

Taurus

Canis Minor

Cetus

Eridanus

Lepus

Canis Major

Fornax

Puppis

This big dog is one of Orion's faithful hunting companions who follows Orion across the sky. He seems to be chasing down Lepus the hare.

Horologium

Carina

19

The Solar System

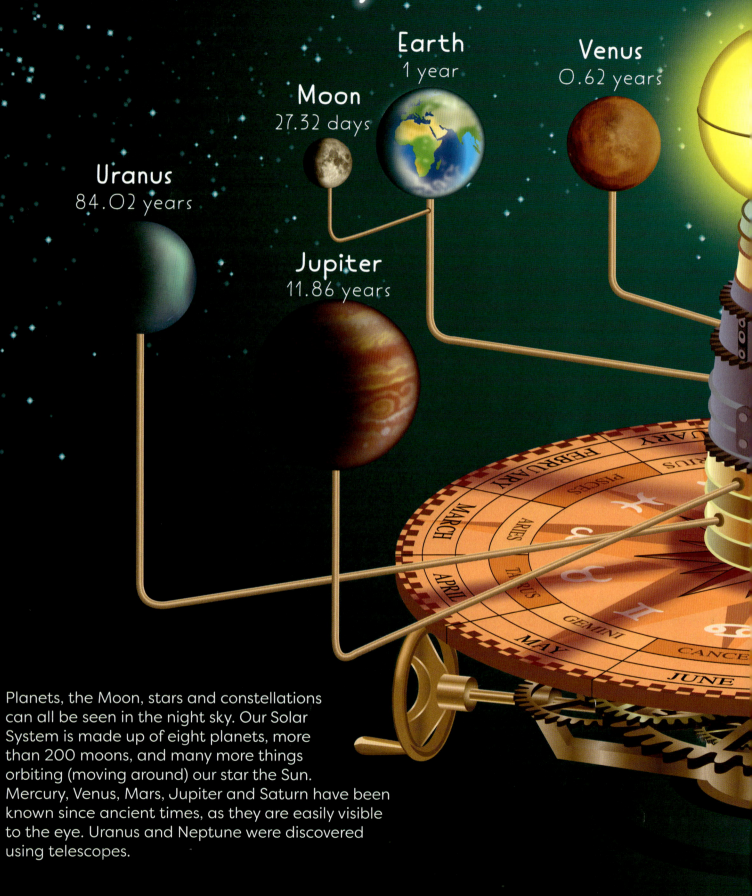

Uranus
84.02 years

Moon
27.32 days

Earth
1 year

Venus
0.62 years

Jupiter
11.86 years

Planets, the Moon, stars and constellations can all be seen in the night sky. Our Solar System is made up of eight planets, more than 200 moons, and many more things orbiting (moving around) our star the Sun. Mercury, Venus, Mars, Jupiter and Saturn have been known since ancient times, as they are easily visible to the eye. Uranus and Neptune were discovered using telescopes.

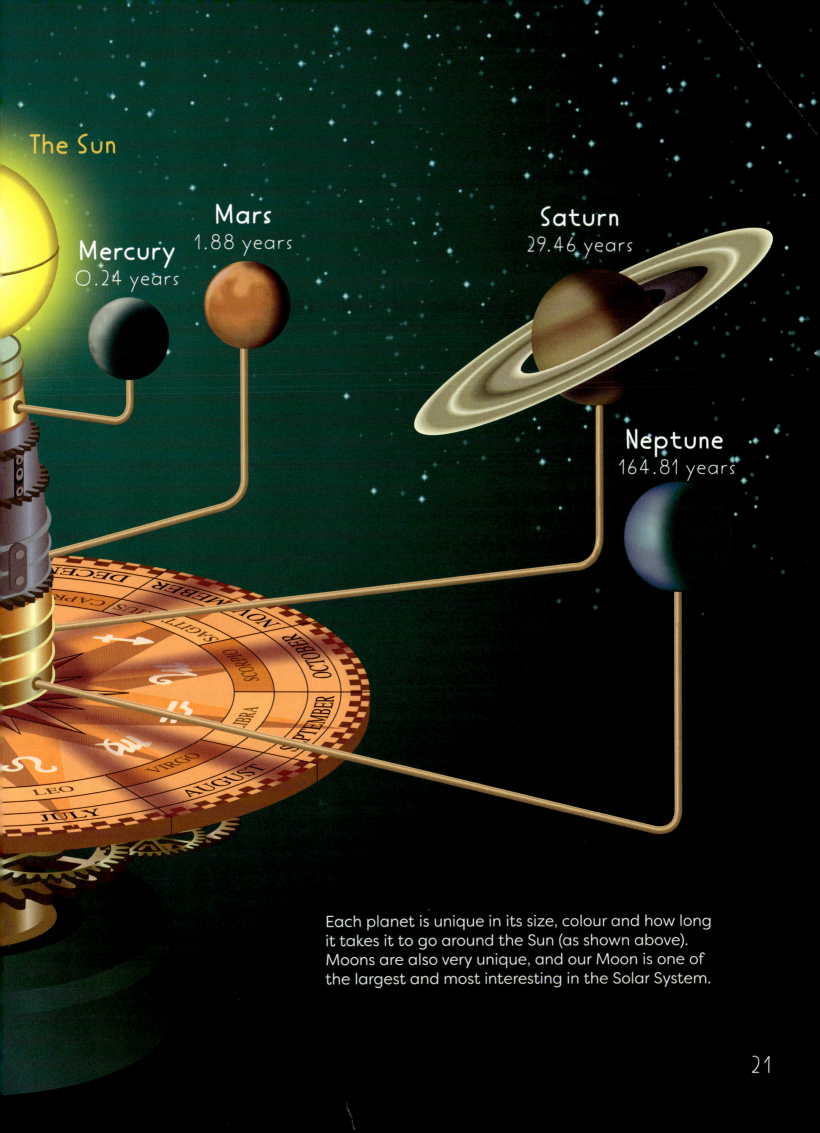

The Sun

Mars
1.88 years

Mercury
0.24 years

Saturn
29.46 years

Neptune
164.81 years

Each planet is unique in its size, colour and how long it takes it to go around the Sun (as shown above). Moons are also very unique, and our Moon is one of the largest and most interesting in the Solar System.

Snakes and Scales

Boötes

Lyra

Corona Borealis

In a classical Greek story, the god Dionysus gifted a crown to Princess Ariadne of Crete. She placed it into the sky creating this little constellation known as Corona Borealis – 'northern crown'.
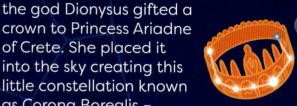

Sometimes Ophiuchus is called the thirteenth constellation of the zodiac because the Sun passes in front of it. In ancient Greece, Ophiuchus was the god Apollo.

Serpens Caput

Serpens

Ophiuchus

Serpens Cauda

Imagine wrestling a giant snake! That's what Ophiuchus (the serpent bearer) is doing. The snake is separated into two halves – Serpens Caput (the snake's head) and Serpens Cauda (the snake's tail).

Scutum

Sagittarius

Scorpius

Antares

Lupus

Corona Australis

Antares is a supergiant star in Scorpius more than 600 times larger than the Sun! It glows with a red-orange colour, and its name means 'rival of Mars', as it looks similar to the red planet in the sky.

Norma

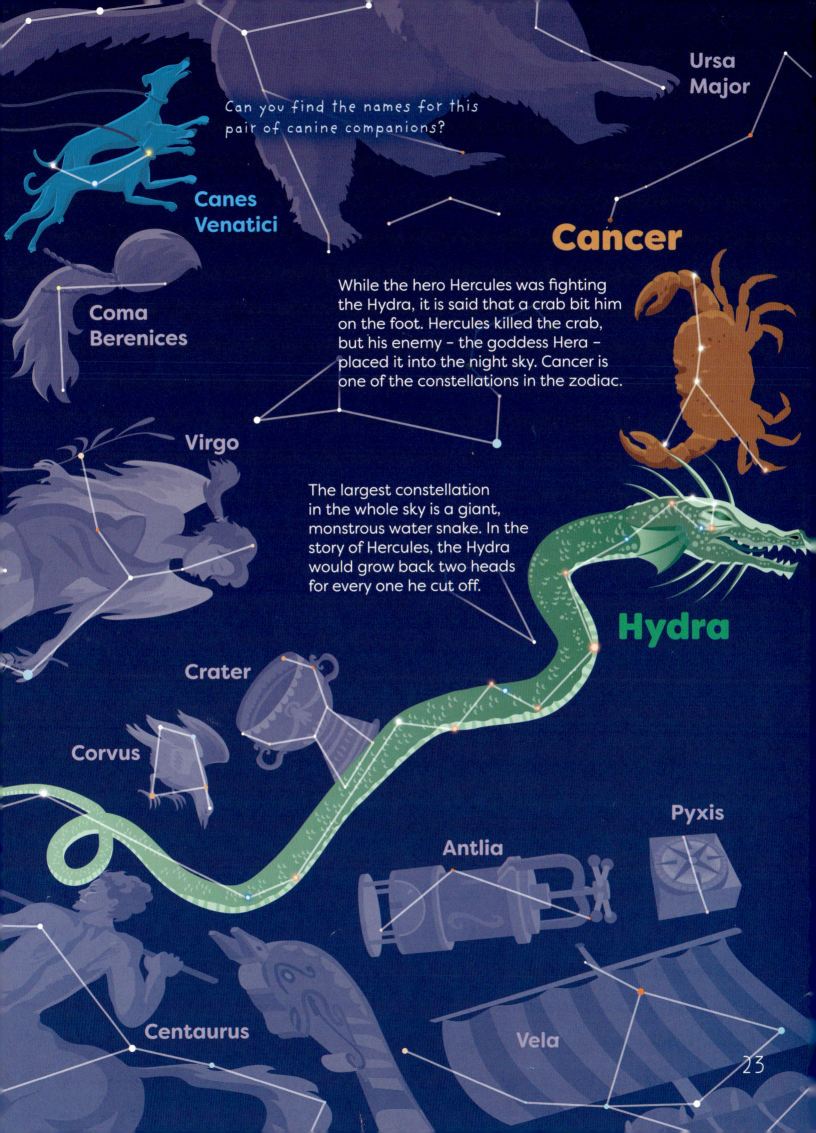

Ursa Major

Can you find the names for this pair of canine companions?

Canes Venatici

Coma Berenices

Cancer

While the hero Hercules was fighting the Hydra, it is said that a crab bit him on the foot. Hercules killed the crab, but his enemy – the goddess Hera – placed it into the night sky. Cancer is one of the constellations in the zodiac.

Virgo

The largest constellation in the whole sky is a giant, monstrous water snake. In the story of Hercules, the Hydra would grow back two heads for every one he cut off.

Hydra

Crater

Corvus

Pyxis

Antlia

Centaurus

Vela

23

Large and Small

All of the 88 constellations are different sizes. Some are very large and others are much smaller.

Hydra

The largest constellation is Hydra, a giant water monster snaking across the sky.

The smallest constellation is Crux, which is also called the Southern Cross. We measure the size of constellations by how much area they take up in the sky. Crux could fit into Hydra 19 times!

Crux

Fox and Fish

Not far from Cygnus is faint little Lacerta the lizard. This constellation was introduced by Johannes Hevelius, a famous Polish astronomer, in the 17th century. He wanted to place the 'starred agama', or 'star lizard' in the sky. It is found in parts of Asia, the Middle East and Africa.

Lacerta

Andromeda

Vulpecula

Vulpecula the fox isn't associated with an ancient myth. Can you make one up?

Pisces

This pair of fish in the zodiac represents the goddess Aphrodite and her son Eros, who were transformed into fish so that they could hide in a river from the monster Typhon.

Delphinus

Equuleus

This pattern used to be called 'apparatus sculptoris', which means the 'sculptor's studio'. Humans have been making sculptures for over ten thousand years!

Piscis Austrinus (the southern fish) is an ancient constellation from the story of Atargatis – a Syrian goddess who fell into a lake and was saved by a large fish.

Capricornus

Sculptor

Piscis Austrinus

Microscopium

Phoenix

Grus

Indus

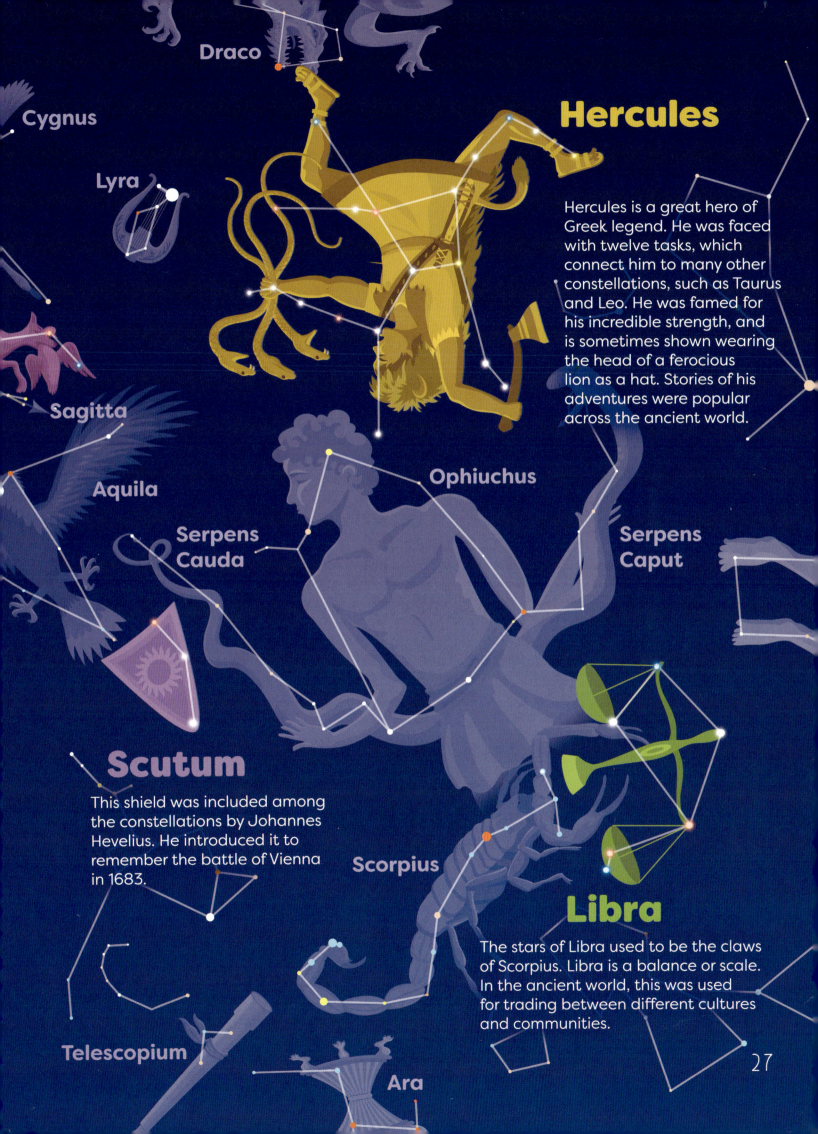

Draco

Cygnus

Lyra

Sagitta

Aquila

Hercules

Hercules is a great hero of Greek legend. He was faced with twelve tasks, which connect him to many other constellations, such as Taurus and Leo. He was famed for his incredible strength, and is sometimes shown wearing the head of a ferocious lion as a hat. Stories of his adventures were popular across the ancient world.

Serpens Cauda

Ophiuchus

Serpens Caput

Scutum

This shield was included among the constellations by Johannes Hevelius. He introduced it to remember the battle of Vienna in 1683.

Scorpius

Libra

The stars of Libra used to be the claws of Scorpius. Libra is a balance or scale. In the ancient world, this was used for trading between different cultures and communities.

Telescopium

Ara

Cosmic Aquarium

Look up at the night sky and you will find many kinds of aquatic animals, both large and small. Sailors used to tell stories about the creatures they saw at sea, and they would find their way home by using the stars at night. Some of the beasts of the sea must have seemed like monsters from a distance!

Cetus

Piscis Austrinus

Delphinus

Pisces

Cetus is commonly shown as a sea monster such as the kraken from the story of the hero Perseus and Princess Andromeda, but the name Cetus actually means 'whale'. Ancient sailors may have mistaken whales for sea monsters, inspiring many stories about this constellation.

Hydrus

Volans

How many of these creatures have you seen in the sea or the sky?

Dorado

Cancer

Hunter and Hero

Perseus

Taurus

Pleiades

Gemini

Cetus

Orion

The legendary Greek hunter Orion claimed he could kill any animal, but his fate was sealed by Scorpius the scorpion. He is shown in the sky fighting Taurus the bull to try and save seven beautiful sisters, marked by the Pleiades star cluster.

Sirius is the brightest star in the whole sky! It is found in Canis Major and is close to the Sun.

Canis Major

Sirius

Lepus

Fornax

Columba

Columba was originally called Columba Noachi ('Noah's dove'). In the biblical story of Noah's ark, a dove revealed to Noah that the great flood was coming to an end.

Andromeda

Lacerta

Cygnus

Triangulum

In one of the great stories of the sky, the hero Perseus saved the princess Andromeda from a terrible fate, after she was sacrificed to the sea monster, the kraken. Perseus used the head of Medusa, whose hair was made of snakes, to turn the kraken into stone. The story involves other constellations, including Cassiopeia (queen), Cepheus (king) and the hero's trusty steed Pegasus (winged horse). Can you find these patterns elsewhere in this book?

Aquarius is the cup-bearer of the gods in Greek mythology, but he has also been seen as the god of the Nile by the Egyptians. He is shown pouring water or nectar into the mouth of the Piscis Austrinus. Aquarius is one of the constellations of the zodiac.

Equuleus

Aquarius

Capricornus

What makes the Phoenix a legendary creature?

Phoenix

Fomalhaut

Piscis Austrinus

The name of this star means the 'mouth of the fish'. It is very interesting to astronomers, who have discovered that it is a very young star. It is surrounded by dusty rings and may one day form its own Solar System.

Jewels of Orion

The mighty hunter Orion is one of the most striking constellations. He contains bright and colourful stars including Betelgeuse, which appears orange in the night sky.

Meissa

Bellatrix

Betelgeuse

Orion's Belt

Mintaka

Alnitak

Alnilam

The three stars of Orion's Belt form a straight line, but they are not as close together as they appear. The star in the middle, Alnilam, is much further away than the other two. Its name describes the whole belt, meaning a 'string of pearls'. The stars in Orion's Belt point to the Pleiades star cluster and the brightest star in the night sky, Sirius, which is found in the constellation Canis Major.

Saiph

Rigel

Orion's Sword

Flame
Nebula

Orion's
Belt

Horsehead
Nebula

Running
Man Nebula

Orion's
Sword

The Orion
Nebula

Several beautiful nebulae can be seen near Orion's Belt. A nebula is a
cloud of gas in space. These nebulae glow because of the energy they
receive from nearby stars. The Orion Nebula in the centre of Orion's
Sword contains many baby stars, causing it to glow bright enough to
be visible to the eye on a dark night. Many nebulae take their names
from their appearance in binoculars or telescopes – for example, the
Horsehead Nebula reminded people of a knight chess piece.

Cross and Canines

Sextans looks like a sextant, which is an important tool that was once used by astronomers to measure stars in the sky. It is still used today for navigation at sea.

Sextans

This crow (or raven) was the sacred bird of Apollo, the god of the Sun. It once had white feathers, but when Apollo became angry with Corvus, he scorched them black.

Crater

Hydra

In Greek mythology, the Argo Navis is the ship that the group of heroes called the Argonauts travelled on. It was also once thought to be the boat of the god Osiris by Egyptian storytellers. Argo Navis is made up of three constellations: Carina, Puppis and Vela.

Pyxis

Corvus

Argo Navis

Vela

Carina

Crux, also called the Southern Cross, is the smallest constellation. It is seen across the southern hemisphere, and it appears on the Australian flag.

What are wolves thought to howl at in the night sky?

Lupus

Crux

Musca

Circinus

Chamaeleon

Apus

Canis Minor

Lepus has been seen for thousands of years as a hare. It is being chased by Orion's hunting dogs – Canis Major and Canis Minor – across the sky.

Orion

Taurus

Lepus

Can you see the V-shaped star cluster in the bull's head? This is called the Hyades.

Canis Major

Puppis

Columba

Eridanus

Cetus

Canopus

Canopus, a star in Carina, is the second brightest star in the sky.

Fornax

Volans

Across the ancient world in many cultures, people spoke of a mythical bird with fiery feathers. It could live for hundreds of years, before it would burn away in a blaze of fire. From the ashes, a new bird would be born.

Mensa

Hydrus

Phoenix

Sailing and the Stars

Pleiades
star cluster

Vela

Carina

Delphinus

Argo Navis

Dorado

Pyxis

People have a long history of navigating using the stars. This was very important during the Age of Sail, when it became possible to travel great distances over the sea using large ships. In Ancient Greece, sailors would look to see the Pleiades star cluster rising before sunrise, and they knew this was the beginning of the sailing season in the Mediterranean Sea. Many constellations celebrate our long history of sailing, including the great ship Argo Navis, Pyxis the compass and a variety of wonderful sea life that sailors became familiar with. Once one large constellation, Argo Navis has since been broken into several smaller constellations representing parts of the ship – Puppis the stern, Carina the keel and Vela the sail.

Puppis

Volans

Claws and Cup

Ophiuchus

Serpens Cauda

Scutum

This constellation of the zodiac is a goat fish. In this legend, a man with the legs and horns of a goat, called Pan, jumped into a river to escape the monster Typhon and transformed into Capricornus the goat fish.

Capricornus

Corona Australis means 'southern crown'. Unlike Princess Ariadne's northern crown, this one does not have a classical story, but it is very ancient.

Corona Australis

Aquarius

Norma

Telescopium

Ara

Microscopium

Triangulum Australe

Indus

Piscis Austrinus

Apus

Indus may have been inspired by the indigenous Madagascan people, who were met by Dutch sailors when they travelled to Indonesia in the late 16th Century.

Sculptor

Octans

Tucana

Boötes

Serpens Caput

Which pair of animals does Boötes look after?

Coma Berenices

Look at the red star, Antares, at the heart of Scorpius. Which planet does it remind you of?

Scorpius

Crater is the cup of the god Apollo and is part of a strange story. Apollo sent his crow (Corvus) to fetch water in his cup, but the bird got distracted by a fig tree and feasted on the figs. When Corvus finally returned with the cup of water, the angry (and very thirsty) Apollo cast them into the sky!

In Greek mythology, Chiron was a centaur with the head of a man and body of a horse. He taught heroes like Hercules and Perseus.

Crater

Centaurus

Lupus

Corvus

Sextans

Antlia

Antlia the air pump is one of a few scientific instruments in the night sky. It is not ancient, but was created a few hundred years ago.

Alpha Centauri

Crux

Centaurus is home to the nearest star in the sky – Alpha Centauri.

Pyxis

Vela

Carina

Chamaeleon

Heroes and Villains

Our ancestors loved to tell inspiring stories about great heroes, some of which appear among the constellations. Of course, great heroes also need great villains to do battle with. In some cases, they are monstrous creatures of legend. In others, familiar animals played the roles of the baddies.

Auriga

Pegasus

Perseus

Orion

Sagittarius

Hercules

Gemini

Which do you think is the bravest hero, and which do you think is the most ferocious villain?

According to legend, the hero Hercules defeated a lion, which we see as Leo. He also fought with a crab (Cancer) and captured a bull (Taurus) who was the father of the Minotaur, a mythical creature with the head and tail of a bull and the body of a man. The mighty hunter Orion was said to have been killed by a scorpion (Scorpius) after becoming too boastful.

Hydra

Cetus

Cancer

Taurus

Scorpius

Leo

41

Wings and Water

The river Eridanus may take its name from the ancient city Eridu. Greek storytellers spoke of a being called Phaëton, who was struck by a lightning bolt from the god Zeus, and jumped into this river to put out the fire in his hair.

Eridanus

Fornax is a young constellation showing a furnace that was used by scientists to heat up chemicals.

Fornax

Sculptor

Achernar

Lepus

Caelum

Canis Major

Achernar is a star that is sometimes used to find the South Pole in the sky.

Dorado is a dolphinfish, also known as a mahi-mahi. These large fish are found around the world in tropical waters.

Pictor

Reticulum

Puppis

Mensa

Dorado

Vela

Carina

Pegasus

Equuleus

Equuleus, the little horse, is a very small but very old constellation. In a Greek myth, Equuleus is the daughter of Chiron, the centaur. Stargazers only imagined her head poking out from behind Pegasus.

Pisces

How many fish can you find in the stars?

Grus is a crane, named after a family of birds known for their long legs and long necks. In Greek mythology, the crane was the sacred bird of the god Hermes, but this constellation was introduced only quite recently by Dutch explorers.

Sagittarius, the archer centaur, who had the head of a man and body of a horse, is one of the constellations of the zodiac. He holds a bow and arrow – a weapon that was very important in the ancient world.

Grus

Sagittarius

Microscopium

Scutum

Indus

Pavo

Tucana

Pavo

Corona Australis

This fancy bird is home to a star that shares its name. Pavo – peacock – is a star that astronomers think is very similar to the Sun. In Greek mythology, the goddess Hera's flying chariot was pulled by beautiful, colourful peacocks.

Octans

Lupus

43

Apus

Triangulum Australe

Starry Birds

Aquila

The night sky is full of feathered friends, several of which we see in our everyday lives, and a few of which are more exotic. Astronomers talk about nine bird constellations – eight of them are real birds, shown here, but one is a mythical bird, the Phoenix. Some of these birds, like Cygnus the swan and Aquila the eagle, appear in ancient stories. Others, such as Pavo the peacock and Tucana the toucan, were first introduced hundreds of years ago after European explorers travelled to other parts of the world.

Grus

Pavo

44

Columba

Tucana

Apus

Corvus

Cygnus

45

Northern Polar Skies

These are the stars seen looking straight up from the North Pole.

Polaris is called the Pole Star and is almost straight above Earth's North Pole, also known as the North Celestial Pole. It can be found in the tip of the tail of Ursa Minor, the little bear. Joining the bears is the bright, snaking constellation of Draco the dragon.

In Greek legend, Hercules confronted this dragon, which guarded a tree of golden apples. Much fainter is the constellation Camelopardalis. Its strange name is a combination of camel and leopard, and it was the common English name for a giraffe in the 19th century.

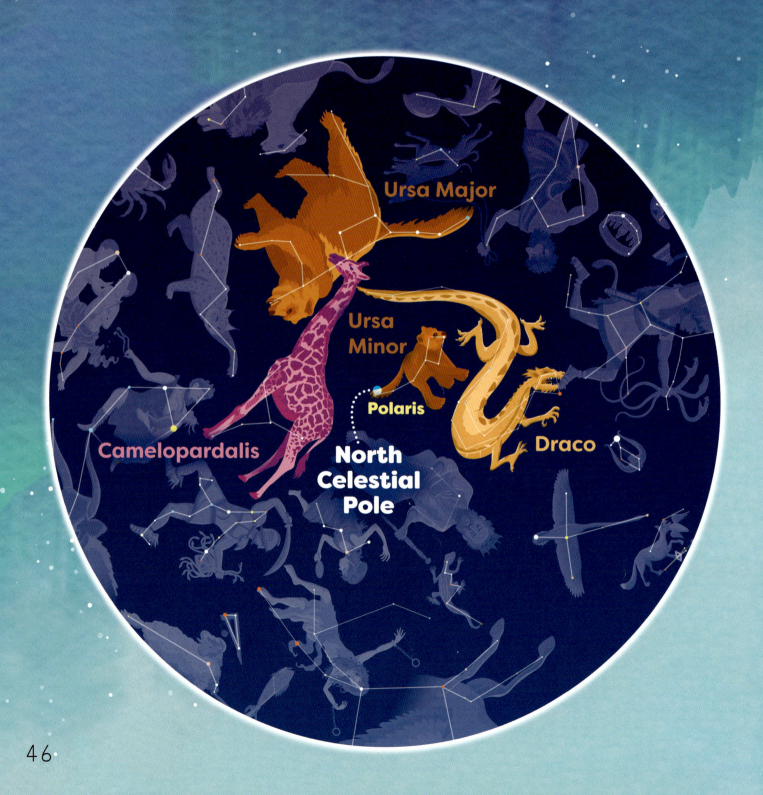

Ursa Major

Ursa Minor

Polaris

North Celestial Pole

Camelopardalis

Draco

Southern Polar Skies

These are the stars seen looking straight up from the South Pole.

There is no bright star marking the point above the Earth's South Pole, also known as the South Celestial Pole, so stargazers have other ways of measuring where true south is. The South Celestial Pole is in the constellation of Octans the octant, an instrument used to help navigation. Nearby is Chamaeleon, Musca the fly and Mensa, which represents Table Mountain in South Africa. The French astronomer Nicolas-Louis de Lacaille created Mensa and Octans when he was studying the stars in Cape Town.

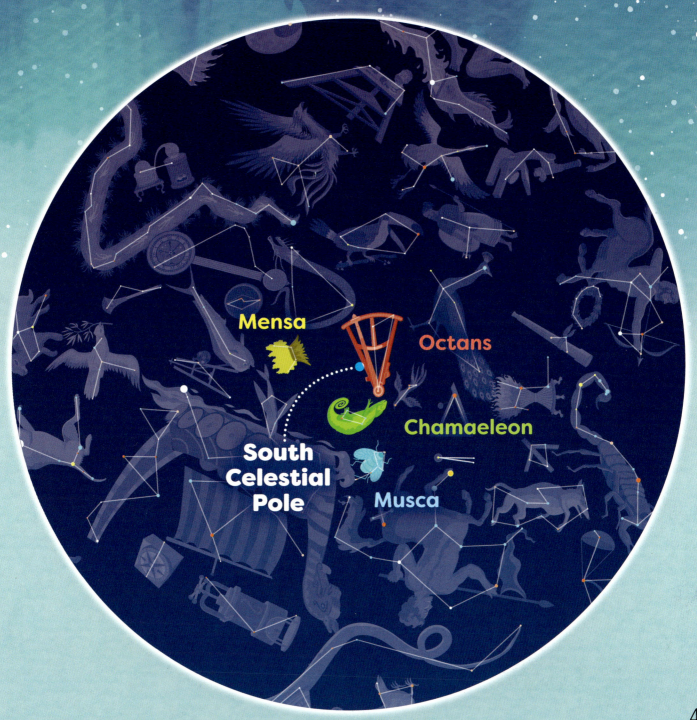

Mensa

Octans

Chamaeleon

South Celestial Pole

Musca

Glossary

constellation A group of stars that form a pattern. Many of the constellations were first identified thousands of years ago.

equator An imaginary line shown on maps that separates the northern hemisphere and the southern hemisphere. The Earth has an equator, and so does the sky.

nebula (plural nebulae) A cloud of gas in space. These giant clouds often glow because they reflect the light of stars, or because they are heated up by stars. Stars are born inside nebulae.

northern hemisphere The northern half of planet Earth, so every part of the world that is north of the equator.

Polaris The proper name for the North Star or Pole Star. Polaris points the way to true north for stargazers in the northern hemisphere.

southern hemisphere The southern half of planet Earth, so every part of the world that is south of the equator.

star chart A map of the stars showing where they appear in the sky. Early star charts were made by hand but today they are made using computers and are very accurate.

star cluster A group of stars that are close together in space. The Pleiades is a very famous star cluster. The Plough (or Big Dipper) is another bright star cluster.

supergiant star A star that is much larger than the Sun. Some of the brightest stars we see in the sky are supergiant stars.

zodiac A collection of twelve constellations that form a band around the sky. Thousands of years ago, they were used as a calendar to track the progress of the seasons.

Constellation index